GRAPHIC SCIENCE

THE EXPLOSIVE WORLD OF VOLCANOES

WITH MAX AXIOM SUPER SCIENTIST

Christopher Harbo

illustrated by Tod Smith

www.raintreepublishers.co.uk
Visit our website to find out
more information about
Raintree books.

To order:
☎ Phone +44 (0) 1865 888066
🖷 Fax +44 (0) 1865 314091
🖳 Visit www.raintreepublishers.co.uk

Raintree is an imprint of Capstone Global Library Limited, a company incorporated in England and
Wales having its registered office at 7 Pilgrim Street, London EC4V 6LB
Registered company number: 6695882

Text © Capstone Press 2008
First published by Capstone Press in 2008
First published in hardback in the United Kingdom by Capstone Global Library in 2010
First published in paperback in the United Kingdom by Capstone Global Library in 2011
The moral rights of the proprietor have been asserted.

ISBN 978 1 406 21461 1 (hardback)   ISBN 978 1 406 21477 2 (paperback)
14 13 12 11 10   15 14 13 12 11

British Library Cataloguing in Publication Data
Harbo, Christopher
Volcanoes. -- (Graphic science)
551.2'1-dc22

A full catalogue record for this book is available from the British Library.

Art Director: Bob Lentz
Designers: Thomas Emery and Kyle Grenz
Colourist: Matt Webb
UK Editor: Diyan Leake
UK Production: Alison Parsons
Originated by Capstone Global Library
Printed and bound in China by South China Printing Company Limited

Disclaimer
All the Internet addresses (URLs) given in this book were valid at the time of going to press.
However, due to the dynamic nature of the Internet, some addresses may have changed, or sites may
have changed or ceased to exist since publication. While the publisher regrets any inconvenience this
may cause readers, no responsibility for any such changes can be accepted by the publisher.

CONTENTS

Super Scientist Max Axiom begins his exploration of volcanoes on the slopes of Arenal in Costa Rica.

One more temperature reading should do the trick.

1500°C

Just as I thought. This lava is hot enough to melt glass.

5

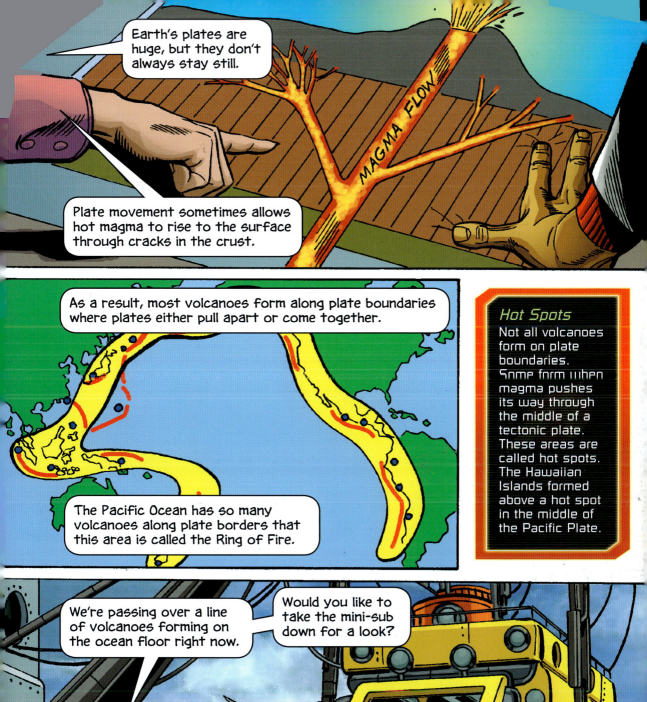

Earth's plates are huge, but they don't always stay still.

Plate movement sometimes allows hot magma to rise to the surface through cracks in the crust.

MAGMA FLOW

As a result, most volcanoes form along plate boundaries where plates either pull apart or come together.

The Pacific Ocean has so many volcanoes along plate borders that this area is called the Ring of Fire.

Hot Spots

Not all volcanoes form on plate boundaries. Some form when magma pushes its way through the middle of a tectonic plate. These areas are called hot spots. The Hawaiian Islands formed above a hot spot in the middle of the Pacific Plate.

We're passing over a line of volcanoes forming on the ocean floor right now.

Would you like to take the mini-sub down for a look?

I sure would!

With 70 percent of the earth covered by water, most volcanoes are hidden deep under the oceans.

But the deepest, darkest place on earth gives us stunning views of newly forming volcanoes.

For instance, here we see how all volcanoes begin with a main vent.

This pipeline to the magma chamber allows hot gases and magma to travel from miles under the crust.

The earth has thousands of volcanoes, but few of them are active.

So, what is an active volcano?

In any given year, 50 to 70 volcanoes erupt around the world.

But erupting volcanoes are not the only ones considered active. Scientists consider any volcano that has erupted in the last thousand years to be active. Active volcanoes also show signs of molten magma beneath them.

By this measure, earth has about 550 active volcanoes.

Of course, most active and inactive volcanoes sit quietly year after year.

Scientists often label these sleeping giants as either dormant or extinct.

A dormant volcano is capable of erupting, but hasn't for many years.

An extinct volcano hasn't erupted in many thousands of years and isn't expected to erupt again.

Japan's Mount Fuji is a dormant volcano that hasn't erupted since 1708.

Hawaii's Kohala volcano hasn't erupted for 60,000 years. At this time, scientists believe it's extinct.

Of course, no one knows for sure when a dormant volcano may erupt or if an extinct volcano is really extinct.

Sleeping giants sometimes wake up.

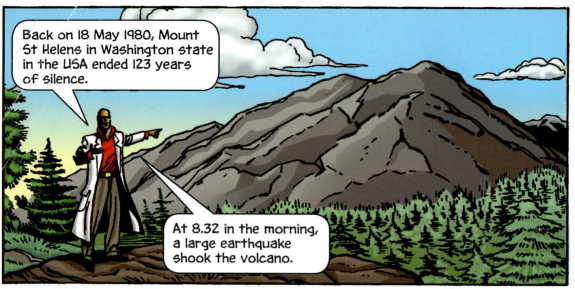

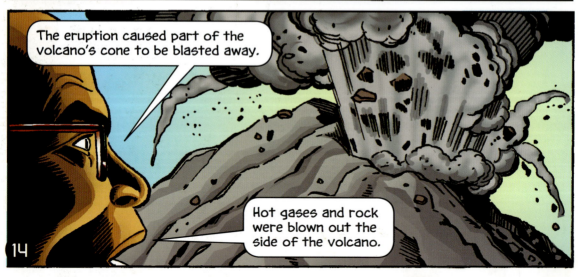

14

Hot gases in magma shattered some of the rock into billions of tiny pieces. These pieces formed ash.

Larger rocks and boulders, called volcanic blocks, were flung from the volcano.

Mixed together, the searing gases, ash, and cinders created a pyroclastic flow. This deadly cloud raced down the volcano and flattened everything in its path.

Mount St Helens' pyroclastic flow destroyed almost 390 square kilometres of forest. That's about 150 square miles.

It killed thousands of animals and 57 people near the volcano.

MUD SLIDES

A mud slide is one of the biggest dangers of a volcanic eruption. Mud slides form when pyroclastic flows melt snow near the top of a volcano. This flow also forms when heavy rains sweep huge amounts of steaming rock, debris, and water down the side of a volcano.

Of course, volcanic eruptions are most famous for spewing red-hot lava.

Let's visit a scientist who spends her days studying lava from Hawaii's Kilauea volcano.

Kilauea is putting on quite a show, Dr. Maka.

Yes, Kilauea has produced a lot of lava for me to study since this eruption began in 1983.

In fact, the rock we're standing on is made of lava. After it flowed down from Kilauea's vent, the lava cooled and hardened.

This fresh lava must be one of the two types of lava flows that have Hawaiian names.

That's right. This lava flow is known as pahoehoe.

"Pa-hoy-hoy." That's fun to say.

And it's more fun to watch.

Pahoehoe flows smoothly and looks like twisted rope when it cools.

While pahoehoe is smooth, another type of lava flow has a very different look.

This must be a'a' lava.

Pronounced "ah-ah," this lava is thicker than pahoehoe.

When it cools, a'a' is jagged and sharp.

Lava flows slowly, but it can cover long distances.

Yes. This black sand is lava that shattered into tiny glass particles when it met the cool ocean.

Cool!

Scientists classify volcanoes by the shape of their cones.

As it turns out, the type of material a volcano ejects has a lot to do with how it looks.

Mauna Loa is a great example.

Like many of the Hawaiian Island volcanoes, Mauna Loa is a shield volcano.

Shield volcanoes are made of very fluid lava and usually release little rock or ash.

As a result, shield volcanoes are dome-shaped. They have gradual slopes because liquid lava flows down rather than building up.

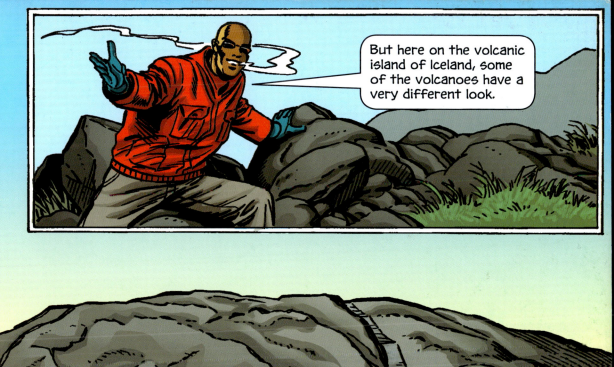

But here on the volcanic island of Iceland, some of the volcanoes have a very different look.

Iceland has many cinder cone volcanoes.

Cinder cones are usually smaller and much steeper than shield volcanoes. They form when globs of lava are thrown into the air by an eruption.

As the lava globs fall, they break apart and cool into cinders that pile up around the volcano's central vent.

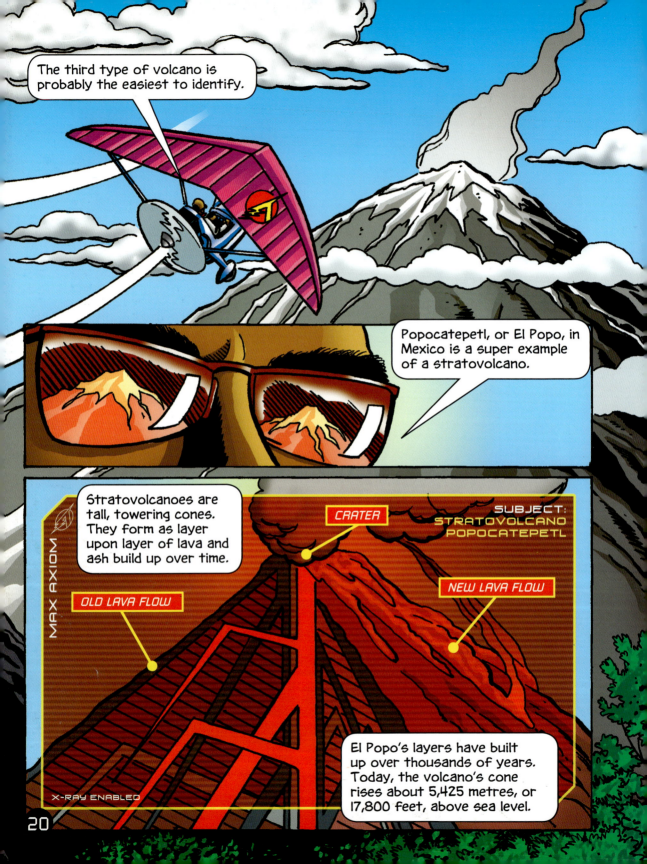

As we've seen, the material erupted has a lot to do with how a volcano looks.

But sometimes eruptions are so violent they tear volcanoes down.

This is Yellowstone National Park in the United States. It's one of the most active calderas in the world.

The Yellowstone region is made up of three overlapping calderas. These calderas formed during massive eruptions 2 million, 1.2 million, and 600,000 years ago.

A caldera is a volcano that lost its upper slopes when they collapsed into the magma chamber during an eruption.

Today, magma beneath Yellowstone's main caldera fuels spectacular geysers, hot springs, and mud pots.

Volcanoes are breathtaking to behold, but the world has seen many deadly eruptions.

Let's visit one of the most devastating eruptions of the 20th century. It happened on the French Caribbean Island of Martinique.

At the start of the 1900s, St Pierre was known as the "Paris of the West Indies".

This busy harbour city was nestled at the base of Mount Pelée.

In early 1902, Mount Pelée began having a series of minor eruptions.

These eruptions alarmed people, but no one expected the tragedy that was about to unfold.

On 8 May, Mount Pelée erupted. A huge glowing cloud of superheated gas, ash, and rock barrelled down on St Pierre at more than 160 kilometres, or 100 miles, per hour.

In less than a minute, the cloud swallowed the city. No one had time to flee.

The cloud's hurricane force caused cement homes and buildings to crumble.

Its Intense heat caused trees and wooden buildings to burst into flames.

The cloud raced into the harbour and destroyed 20 ships.

In an instant, more than 28,000 people were killed.

A shoemaker and a prison inmate were the only two people in the city to escape with their lives.

In all of recorded history, no volcanic event is more famous than the eruption of Italy's Mount Vesuvius in AD 79.

The day was 24 August. It dawned like any other day for the people living in nearby Pompeii.

At about 1.00 in the afternoon, the people of Pompeii heard a deafening boom.

BLAMM!

Hot ash rained down on the city. Many people fled, but some tried to find safety in their homes.

Then, Vesuvius released a pyroclastic flow that swallowed the city. More than 2,000 people were overcome by the deadly cloud.

By the next morning, Pompeii was buried under more than 3 metres, or 10 feet, of hot ash and rock.

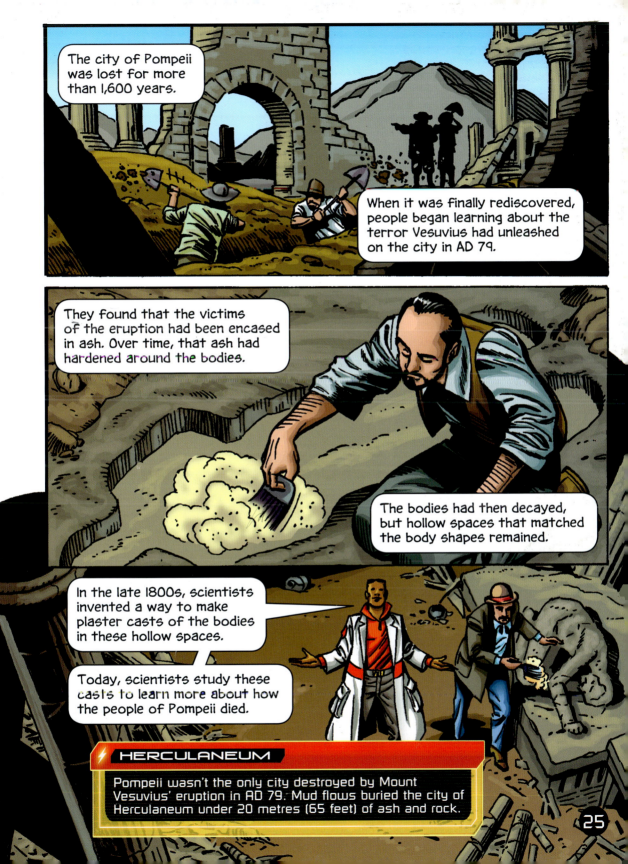

The city of Pompeii was lost for more than 1,600 years.

When it was finally rediscovered, people began learning about the terror Vesuvius had unleashed on the city in AD 79.

They found that the victims of the eruption had been encased in ash. Over time, that ash had hardened around the bodies.

The bodies had then decayed, but hollow spaces that matched the body shapes remained.

In the late 1800s, scientists invented a way to make plaster casts of the bodies in these hollow spaces.

Today, scientists study these casts to learn more about how the people of Pompeii died.

HERCULANEUM

Pompeii wasn't the only city destroyed by Mount Vesuvius' eruption in AD 79. Mud flows buried the city of Herculaneum under 20 metres (65 feet) of ash and rock.

We will be landing at Arenal in about two minutes, Max.

Excellent! Thanks, Sam.

Some scientists learn about volcanoes from past eruptions. Others study them as they erupt.

Scientists who study volcanoes are called volcanologists.

These space-age outfits they sometimes wear help them stay safe near lava flows.

The suits have a metal coating that reflects the intense heat of the lava.

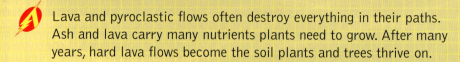

MORE ABOUT VOLCANOES

Lava and pyroclastic flows often destroy everything in their paths. Ash and lava carry many nutrients plants need to grow. After many years, hard lava flows become the soil plants and trees thrive on.

Lava is super hot, but it's not the most dangerous thing a volcano erupts. Lava usually moves so slowly that people have time to get out of its way. Huge mud slides and heated clouds of ash and gases are much more dangerous for people living near an eruption.

In October 2004, Mount St Helens began erupting again. Although the eruptions were minor, the new activity pushed a massive rock slab out of the crater's dome. For a time, the rock slab stood about the length of a football field out of the crater.

In 1991, the eruption of Mount Pinatubo in the Philippines affected the weather around the world. Ash carried worldwide in the air blocked out some sunlight. In the year after the eruption, temperatures around the globe fell an average of 1 degree.

Iceland is one of the few places people can see two of earth's plates spreading apart above sea level. Each year, the plates move apart about 2.5 centimetres (1 inch). As a result, Iceland has many active volcanoes, geysers, and hot springs.

Some scientists use space satellites to study volcanoes. Satellites measure heat released by a volcano and track eruption clouds as they travel around the globe.

Earth isn't the only place in our solar system where volcanoes have formed. Venus, Mars, and Jupiter's moon, Io, also have many volcanoes. In fact, Olympus Mons on Mars is the largest known volcano in the solar system. This huge shield volcano is only slightly smaller than the whole country of Germany. It rises 24 kilometres (15 miles) above the surface of Mars.

 Scientists use an electric thermometer to measure the temperature of lava. This thermometer is made of ceramic and stainless steel. These materials can stand up to lava's high temperatures.

MORE ABOUT

SUPER SCIENTIST

Real name: Maxwell Axiom
Height: 1.86 m (6 ft 1 in.)
Weight: 87 kg (13 st. 10 lb.)
Eyes: Brown   **Hair:** None

Super capabilities: Super intelligence; able to shrink to the size of an atom; sunglasses give X-ray vision; lab coat allows for travel through time and space.

Origin: Since birth, Max Axiom seemed destined for greatness. His mother, a marine biologist, taught her son about the mysteries of the sea. His father, a nuclear physicist and volunteer park warden, showed Max the wonders of the earth and sky.

One day, while Max was hiking in the hills, a megacharged lightning bolt struck him with blinding fury. When he awoke, he discovered a new-found energy and set out to learn as much about science as possible. He travelled the globe studying every aspect of the subject. Then he was ready to share his knowledge and new identity with the world. He had become Max Axiom, Super Scientist.

Glossary

caldera collapsed volcano

cinder cooled piece of lava from an erupting volcano

cone tip of a volcano

crust thin outer layer of the earth's surface

dormant not active. A volcano is said to be dormant if it has not erupted for many years.

erupt suddenly burst. A volcano shoots steam, lava, and ash into the air when it erupts.

extinct no longer active. A volcano is extinct if it has stopped erupting for thousands of years.

lava hot, liquid rock that pours out of a volcano when it erupts

magma melted rock found beneath the surface of the earth

mantle layer of super-hot rock that surrounds the earth's core

molten melted by heat. Lava is molten rock.

plate large sheet of rock that is a piece of the earth's crust

pyroclastic flow moving mixture of hot gases, ash, and rock from a volcano. A pyroclastic flow can reach speeds of up to 160 kilometres (100 miles) per hour.

vent hole in a volcano. Hot ash, steam, and lava blow out of vents from an erupting volcano.

Find Out More

Books

How Does a Volcano Become an Island?, Linda Tagliaferro
(Raintree, 2009)

Into the Fire: Volcanologists, Paul Mason (Heinemann Library, 2007)

Mars (The Universe series), Tim Goss (Heinemann Library, 2007)

Websites

http://news.bbc.co.uk/cbbcnews
Enter "volcanoes" into the Search field to read about how volcanoes
have been in the news.

http://www.nhm.ac.uk/kids-only/
Click on the "Earth and space" tab, then on "Volcanoes" to build a
volcano, learn about lava, and find out more about the role of gases
and water in volcanic eruptions.

INDEX